CW00418691

COMPLETE

Preludes and Fugues for Organ

Johann Sebastian Bach

DOVER PUBLICATIONS, INC.

NEW YORK

Published in Canada by General Publishing Company, Ltd., 30 Lesmill Road, Don Mills, Toronto, Ontario.

Published in the United Kingdom by Constable and Company, Ltd.

This Dover edition, first published in 1985, is a republication of music from two volumes of *Johann Sebastian Bach's Werke*, originally published by the Bach-Gesellschaft in Leipzig. The works on pages 1–122 are from *Joh. Seb. Bach's Orgelwerke. Erster Band* (15th annual Bach-Gesellschaft volume, for 1865, actually 1867; edited by Wilhelm Rust). The works on pages 123–167 are from *Joh. Seb. Bach's Orgelwerke. Dritter Band* (38th annual Bach-Gesellschaft volume, for 1888, actually 1891; edited by Ernst Naumann).

Manufactured in the United States of America

Dover Publications, Inc., 31 East 2nd Street, Mineola, N.Y. 11501

Library of Congress Cataloging in Publication Data

Bach, Johann Sebastian, 1685–1750.

[Organ music. Selections]

Complete preludes and fugues.

Reprint. Originally published: Joh. Seb. Bach's Orgelwerke, Erster, Dritter Band. Leipzig : Bach-Gesellschaft, 1867, 1891.

1. Organ music. 2. Canons, fugues, etc. (Organ)

M10.B 84-759471

ISBN 0-486-24816-X

Contents

(BWV = the catalog number in *Bach-Werke-Verzeichnis*, Leipzig, 1950, . . ., 1966; BG = the volume and page numbers in Bach-Gesellschaft, *Johann Sebastian Bach's Werke*, Leipzig, as described on page iv).

NOTE: The present volume contains only the Prelude/Fugue sets (also called "two-movement" Preludes-and-Fugues). Individual Preludes and individual Fugues for organ will appear in a future Dover volume that will also include Toccatas and Fugues and other organ works.

Two compositions listed in the 1980 *New Grove* as Prelude/Fugue sets are not included here for the following reasons: the Prelude and Fugue set in E-flat Major ("St. Anne," BWV 552) has already been included, as part of the *Clavierübung Part III*, in Dover's volume *Johann Sebastian Bach: Organ Music* (22359-0); the Prelude and Fugue set in E Major (BWV 566) is considered by us, as it is by Schmieder, a Toccata and Fugue set, and is to be included in the above-mentioned future volume.

COMPLETE

Preludes and Fugues for Organ

Prelude and Fugue, C Major (BWV 531)

Fuga.

Prelude and Fugue, D Major (BWV 532)

Alla breve.

Adagio.

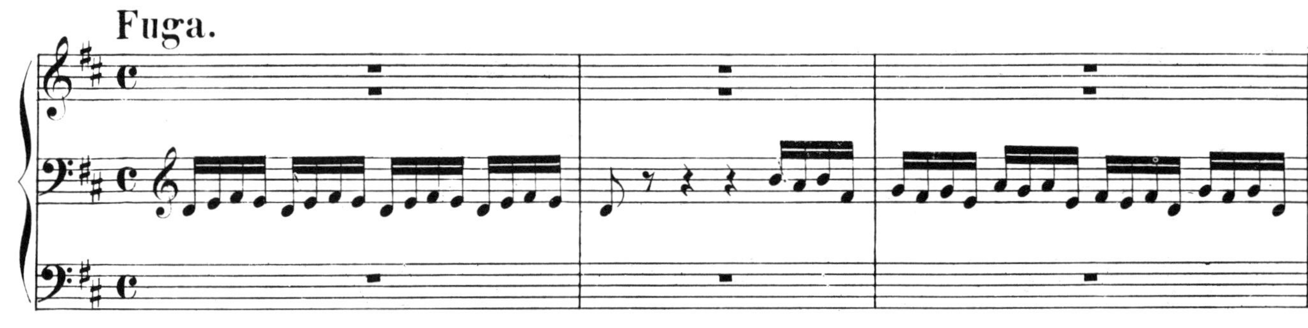

Fuga.

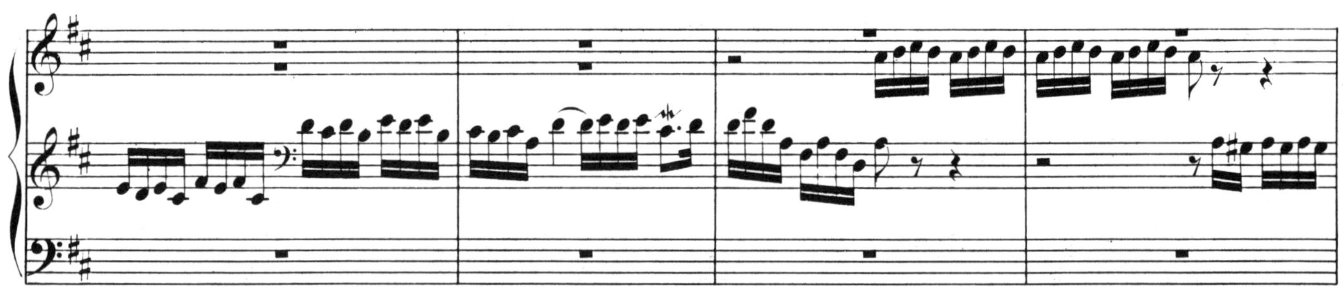

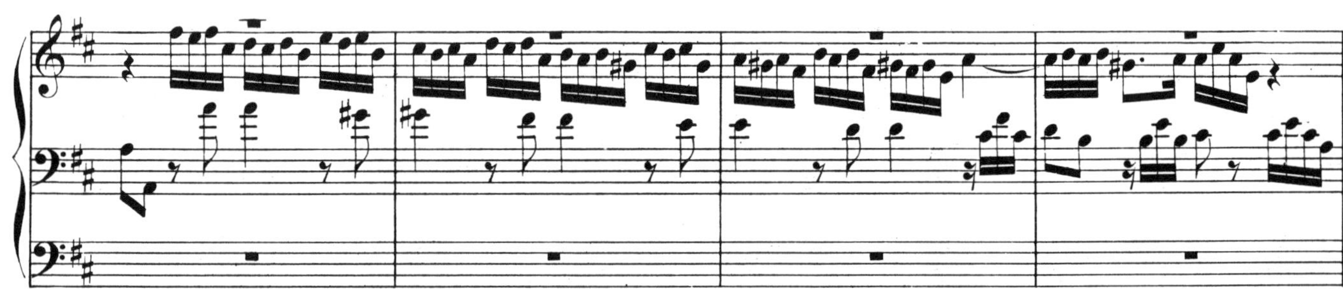

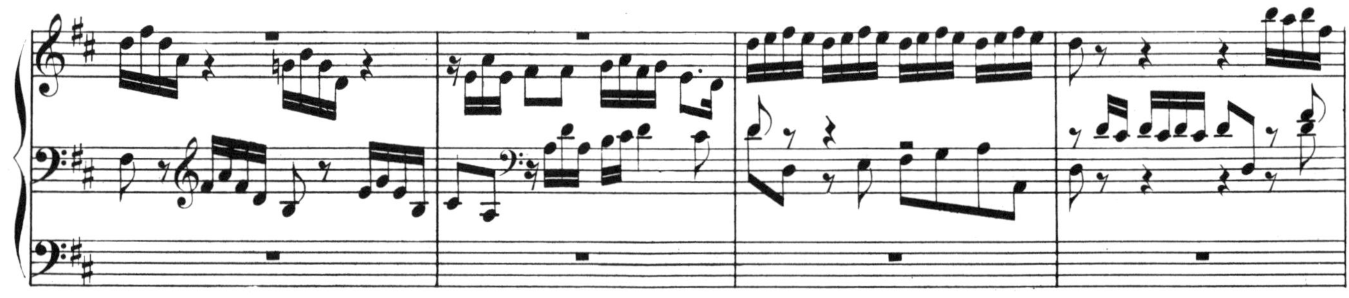

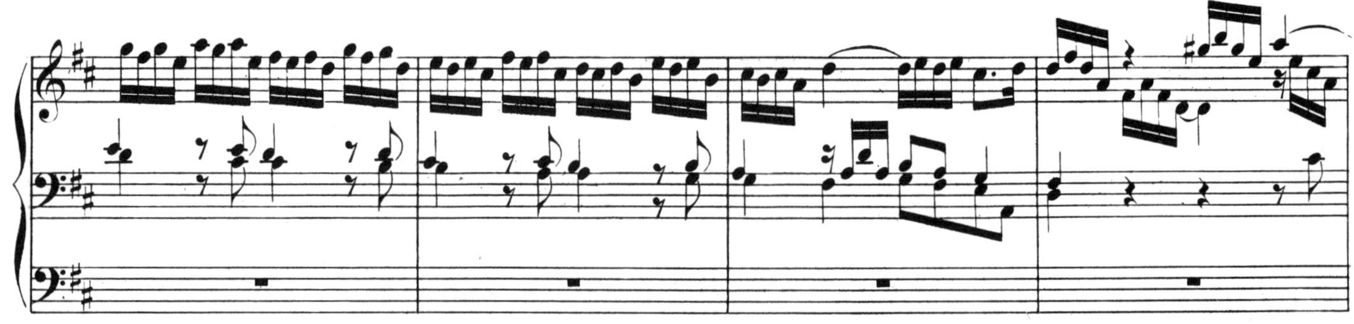

Prelude and Fugue, E Minor (BWV 533)

Fuga.

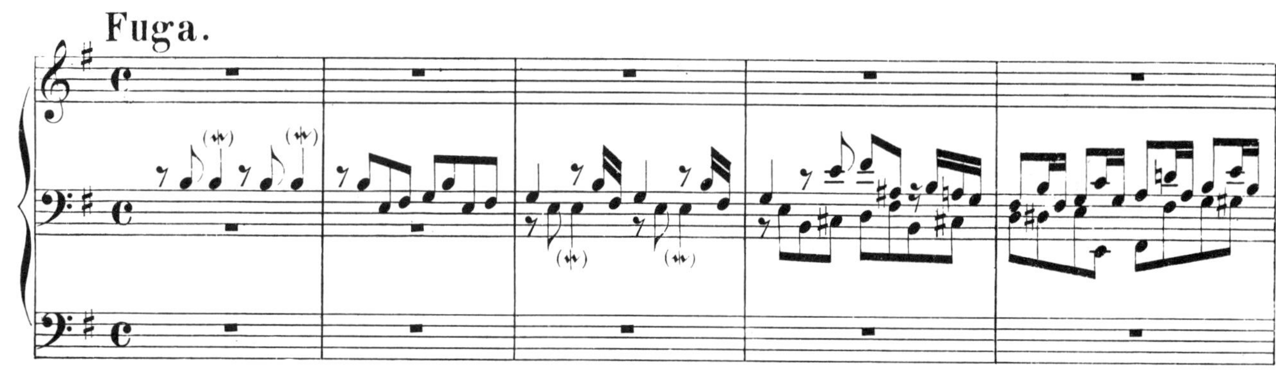

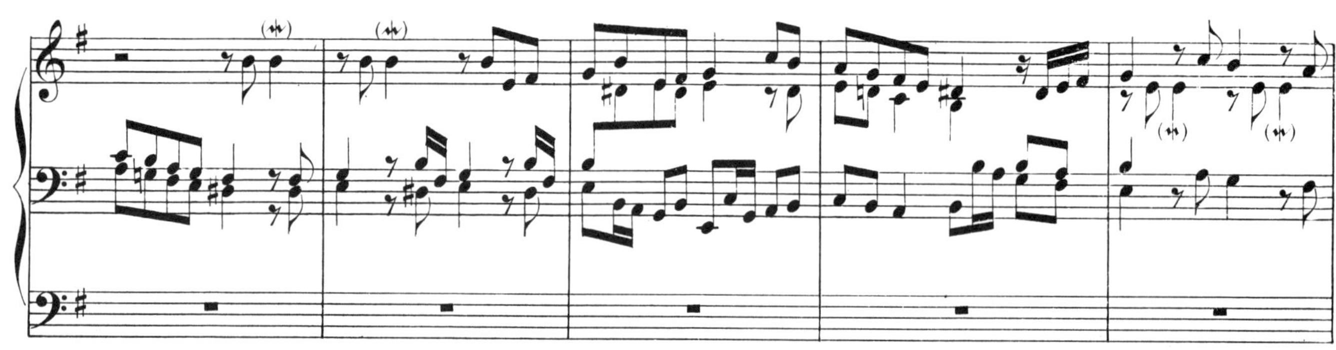

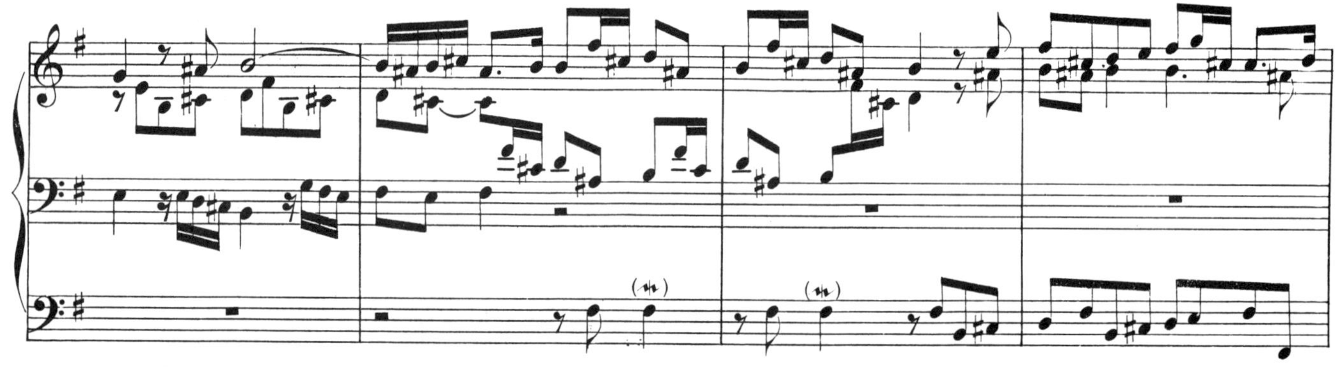

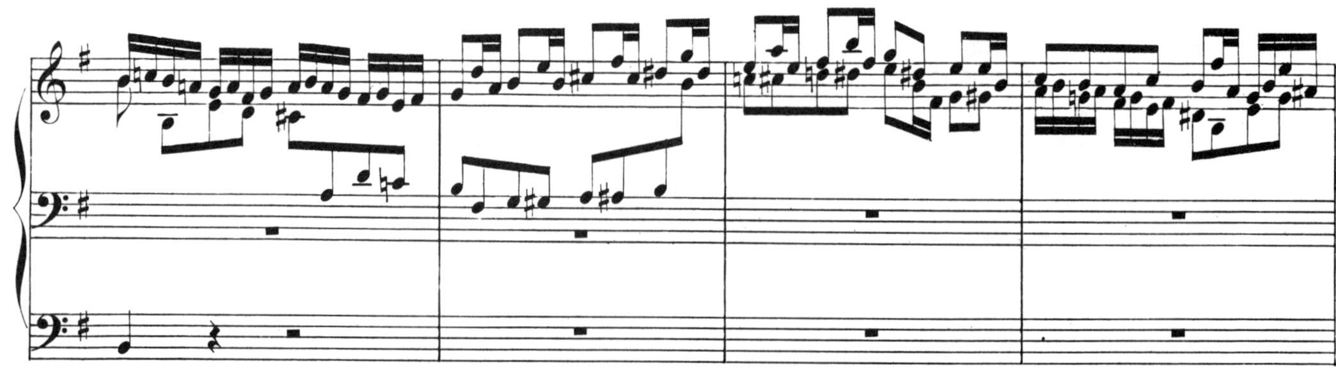

Prelude and Fugue, F Minor (BWV 534)

Praeludium.

Fuga.

tr

Prelude and Fugue, G Minor (BWV 535)

Fuga. Allegro.

(tr)

Prelude and Fugue, A Major (BWV 536)

Fuga.

(w)
(tr)
(tr)

Prelude and Fugue, D Minor (BWV 539)

Fuga.
Manuale.
Pedale.

Prelude and Fugue, G Major (BWV 541)

Fuga.

Prelude and Fugue, A Minor (BWV 543)

Fuga.

6
6
6

Prelude and Fugue, B Minor (BWV 544)

Fuga.

Prelude and Fugue, C Major (BWV 545)

Fuga.

Prelude and Fugue, C Minor (BWV 546)

Fuga.

Prelude and Fugue, C Major (BWV 547)

Praeludium.

Fuga.

oder:

Prelude and Fugue, E Minor (BWV 548)

Fuga.

Prelude and Fugue, C Minor (BWV 549)

Fuga.

tr
(♭)
tr
tr
(𝆖)
tr
tr
tr

Ped.
m. s.
tr

Prelude and Fugue, G Major (BWV 550)

Praeludium.

Fuga.

Alla breve e staccato.

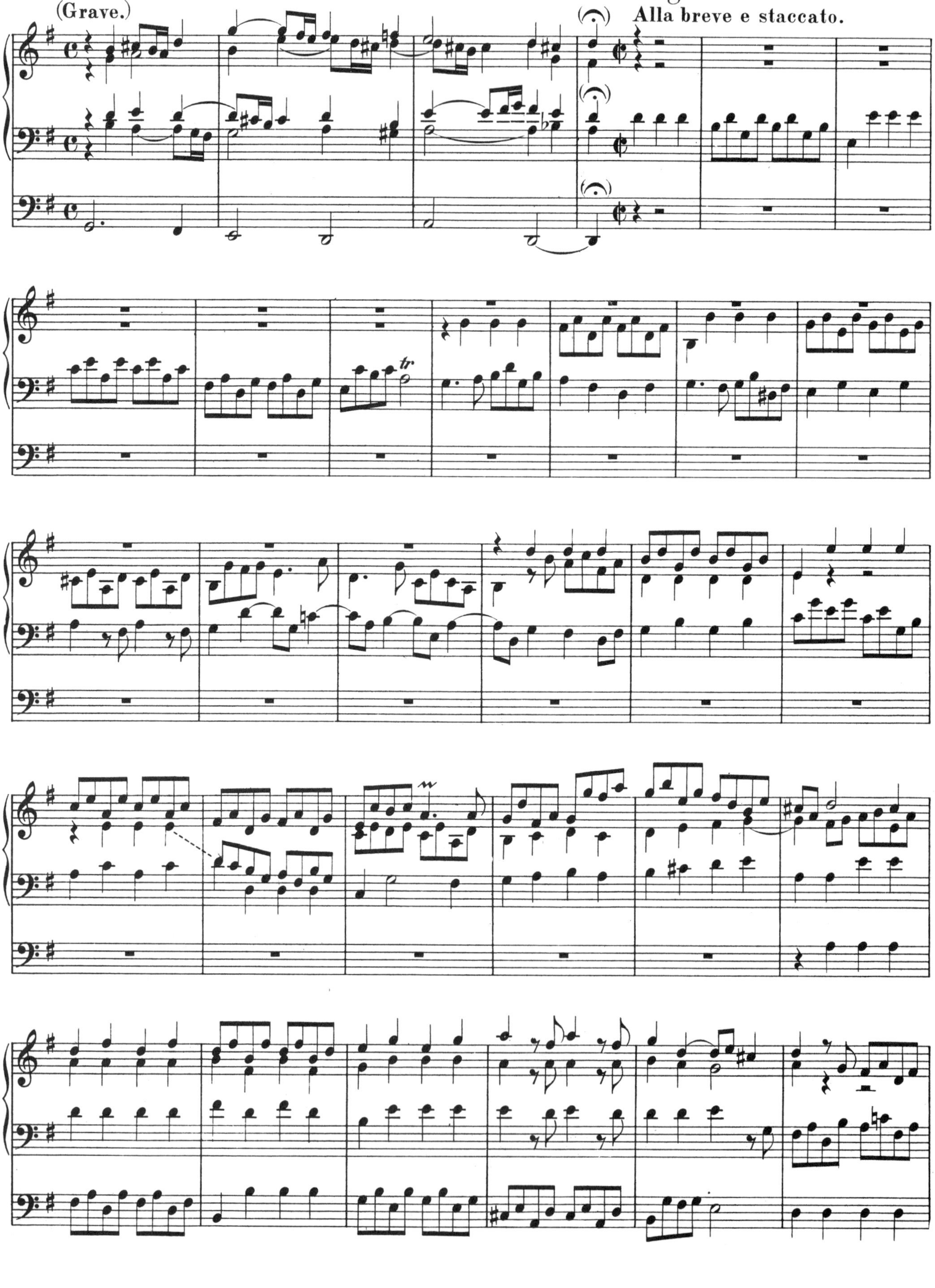

(tr)

Prelude and Fugue, A Minor (BWV 551)

Fuga.

(tr

Eight Short Preludes and Fugues (BWV 553–560)

1ma
2da
Fuga.
tr

tr
tr

2.
Praeludium.
Manual.
Pedal.
tr
tr

Fuga.
tr
tr

3. Praeludium.

Fuga.

4. Praeludium.

Fuga.
tr

tr
tr

Praeludium.

5.

Fuga.
tr

tr
tr
tr

6. Praeludium.

tr
Fuga.
tr

tr

7. Praeludium.

(tr)
(tr)
(tr)
(tr)
(tr)
(tr)
Fuga.
tr

tr

8. Praeludium.

Fuga.
tr

tr
tr